# ABOUT

"Sarah is one of the most deliberate women I know. She has an amazing ability to focus on what is essential and do work that matters-- while always keeping her family as her top priority. I admire her organization skills, her courage, her passion, and her desire to make life better for those around her."

**April Perry, Co-Founder**
**PowerOfMoms.com**

"Sarah is one of those people I look at and wonder if she knows how powerful she really is. She has this huge influence on those that know her and especially those who she mentors and coaches, because she comes from such a deep authentic desire to serve and a high degree of knowledge and experience which allows her to serve with a high level of integrity."

**Gerald Rogers, Author**
**'The Marriage Advice I Wish I Would Have Had'**

In March of 2014 on a hot day in San Diego I was accosted by the blur of a flying object with a whipping braid of dark hair and the scream of excitement. That is my most vivid memory of Sarah Chapman. She had just completed a grueling 5 minute kettlebell snatch test and had sprinted about a hundred yards to celebrate her achievement with me. It wasn't the accomplishment that was so impressive as it was the zeal and tenacity with which she prepared on short notice to pass one of the most difficult certifications in the country.

Just a few weeks earlier I had challenged her to get StrongFirst certified because I could see the passion she had for training with kettlebells. In my mind I was thinking she should wait another 6 months, but that just isn't Sarah. Within a few days of our conversation she was signed up and ready to roll.

This experience encapsulates so many of the great qualities Sarah possesses. I'm not sure any of us, including Sarah, thought she had a realistic chance to pass the cert on such short notice, but she had made up her mind that she was going to give it a shot, pass or fail.

Sarah approaches life's challenges not with an absence of fear and trepidation, but with a resolute ambition to overcome the obstacles that stand in her way. This is what makes her great. She lives in the present. She lives with a positive outlook on life. She doesn't avoid or skirt difficult situations, but steps forward with confidence that whatever is in store will teach her a new lesson that she can share with someone else in need.

Sarah is the kind of person that makes us all better because she is always ready and willing to give back all that she has gleaned from her own experience. I have grown to value her advice and friendship and count her as an important resource to my own success.

**Rob Morris**
**Owner, Lyceum Human Performance**
**2006 NFL Super Bowl Winner**
**Indianapolis Colts 2000-2008**

"Sarah walked into my gym in May 2013 and from the first moment I met her, she stood out. She stood out to me and made an impression for several reasons. First, she herself was a hard worker. She pushed  herself, but also allowed us, as her coaches, to push her and test her limits.

Sarah also made an impression on me and others around her by motivating others in class. Her words of encouragement did, and still do, mean a lot to the members of our gym. She believes in everyone around her and their capabilities. Sarah sees what they can accomplish and encourages them through words and love to reach their goals."

**Trish Allen, Certified Nutritionist**
SpoonsandBells.com
**NPC Bikini Competitor**

Carol,

Oh the experiences we've had together over all these years. So grateful you came into my life when you did. The lessons we've learned together has made us who we are!

This book is about how to control our negative thoughts and have God walk with us out of them.

I know that if you follow the steps and the other tools in this book that you will feel empowered and more confident in who you are as a daughter of God.

I will cherish you forever and your family. So grateful too to share experiences with Jace too.

I love you

Jane

# MINDSTRENGTH

## *for Women*

*How to go from feeling 'insecure', 'judged', and 'not good enough' to getting the body, relationships, and life you want and become "sexy confident."*

## SARAH CHAPMAN

MindStrength for Women

How to go from feeling 'insecure', 'judged', and 'not good enough' to getting the body, relationships, and life you want and become "sexy confident."

Sarah Chapman

Published by Mental Work Publishing

Copyright © Sarah Chapman, 2015

ISBN 0-69237-595-3

Publisher:        Mental Work Publishing
                  220 N 1300 West, Suite 4
                  Pleasant Grove, UT 84062

# ACKNOWLEDGEMENTS

This book comes from my own experiences and also the many hours I've either spent reading about, listening to, or watching mentors that have shown up in my life. These mentors have made me aware of new possibilities. I'd like to personally thank a few of those namely Gerald Rogers, Marci Lock, and Tony & Bri Litster.

Thank you to the women I work with each day through my mentoring program that open their hearts and minds to thinking and digging deep into their inner core to strengthen themselves. It truly is exciting to watch these sisters first start the program broken and hopeless and then see the transformation happen as the weeks progress towards where they are now.

Enormous thanks to Rob Morris, Jesse & Trish Allen, Coach Stevo, and Dan John for introducing me to the art of coaching and believing in me when I didn't. They saw something in me at a time that I couldn't. They continue to lead and guide me through my journey with my body and kettlebell training.

Mom, thank you for always nurturing the family with love, service and devotion. Dad, thanks for always reminding me that I can push a little harder and to change my thinking to what's possible. Your faith in me and your zest for life inspires me.

To my four children, Reeghan, Paetan, Easton, and Stratton, I'm sure this book won't interest you for a while. As your mother, I am already teaching you these tools to help prepare you for what you will experience on this grand experience of life. I love you all to the moon and back and I am ever so grateful to be your mom.

Trent, thank you for helping me uncover these words and for believing in me and wiping away my tears as I wrote this book. You helped turn those tears into peace and clarity. This book is my love song to God, giving thanks for you and who you are as the man in my life!

# CONTENTS

# FOREWORD

It was love at first sight. For me anyway. Apparently the feeling wasn't mutual. I'm grateful that Sarah eventually did fall in love with me and that I was able to persuade her to marry me.

I am Trent Chapman, Sarah Chapman's husband. I asked Sarah to allow me to write the foreword to her book and she hesitated, resisted a little, but then said yes.

The one thing that I think everyone should know about Sarah is that she is a real, imperfect woman. She doesn't pretend to be the perfect wife, mother, daughter, friend or anything else. She is humble in accepting her weaknesses and powerfully accepts her strengths. Some may confuse this acceptance of strength as pride, but those that know Sarah recognize it as confidence.

Why would that be the one thing I want everyone to know about Sarah? I think her confident acceptance of her imperfections as well as her strengths is what makes her so approachable and so real to the women she mentors.

The second thing I think every reader of this book should know about Sarah is that she has overcome a lot of challenges during the last few years. I'm not comparing

Sarah to anyone else as I know there is always someone with bigger and more severe life challenges, but the way she has learned to handle her challenges is inspiring.

Sarah's experience in creating change in her life, and in my life, is what makes her such a powerful mentor and messenger. She went from a quiet, insecure stay at home mom to a woman who stands up and allows her voice to be heard, stands out in the crowd with her sexy confidence and stands strong in her resolve to create the life that she decides.

I know my opinion is heavily biased, but after almost 14 years of marriage I know Sarah's heart better than anyone. I believe Sarah was blessed with a quiet charisma that allows her to assist women of all walks of life to feel God's love. Sarah has a true passion and desire to lead women to God, so they may be filled with His love, to the point that they love themselves.

I would encourage you to pay attention to the ideas and inspiration and "ah-ha" moments as you read. Do not think that you can wait to take action, instead, stop reading and take action immediately in the moment you feel prompted. This approach to living and learning has always served me and I hope it will serve you as well.

# INTRODUCTION

This book is my way of giving hope to women who are feeling like they aren't good enough. Those that are constantly judging themselves, assuming others are always judging them and living a life of trying to please everyone else. This book will share the path I went on from feeling frustrated, unsatisfied, feeling hopeless and unworthy of love or happiness to feeling totally accepted, loved and approved as the wonderfully imperfect version of me on my way to being a better version of me.

The best part is, as soon as I was able to accept the imperfect me, a much better version of me started to come out almost effortlessly in all areas of my life; physically, spiritually, mentally and emotionally!

I lived a very sheltered life growing up. I had an amazing childhood and life was good and safe. I believed that nothing could go wrong. I was a very happy and content child. Looking back, I was naive and didn't know much about the hard parts of life like communication, relationships, my thoughts, etc. I was in la la land.

Where I was in my life seemed like a fairy tale. Then, in my sophomore year of college I left the house for the first time to live on my own. What a slap in the face that was of reality! I knew it would be different, but as time went on, I soon recognized I had lived in a bubble. At home I was told that I was loved, accepted, and approved of, no matter how I dressed, how I did my hair and if I wore makeup or not. I was told at home that I mattered and that I had a purpose.

I entered this new world of living on my own and having new responsibilities. I took difficult classes, had to wake up early, and shop for and make my own food. Then I had to learn how to live with 5 other girls who were not my sisters. In addition to that, I had to worry about men, dating, and wanting a relationship and learning how to deal with feeling rejected.

During my first semester in college I started seeing my weight increase as proper eating habits and a healthy diet became less of a priority. I stayed up late with my roommates and ate whenever I felt like eating. My sleep routine was anything, but consistent. I started to stress about my body weight on a daily basis for the first time in my life. I began telling myself each day as I woke up that I was "frumpy". I started comparing myself to my roommates and it started a negative battle in my mind. As I walked around on campus I would just see girl after girl who seemed to have it all together. I judged more and more. Can you relate to this experience?

I pretended that I was happy and striving to live what I thought was my perfect life, but in reality I was far from living my "perfect life". I started looking to others to tell me whether I measured up. I feared that if I let my true self show, I wouldn't be enough. I couldn't let others think I was anything less than what they expected me to be.

Fast forward one year. I became a wife and then a couple of years later, a mother. I carried these negative thoughts into my marriage. I would find evidence that I "wasn't good enough" whenever I made mistakes. I did things how I thought they were supposed to be, because of outside influences. It consumed my every thought and it drained me so much that I finally threw up my hands and sought out help.

Most women I have mentored have told me that they felt their life has taken a similar path. From being hopeful and happy to frustrated and even miserable. You may be in a situation of a lifeless marriage, a dead end job, or just not happy in the body you're in. Maybe you're trying to figure out what's next in your life. Maybe you're wanting to start developing a talent or follow a passion that you've been putting off. Maybe your laundry is piling up, your car is a filthy mess or your child won't stop crying and you hardly have time to yourself to use the bathroom.

Imagine I'm sitting right in front of you, looking into your eyes. Why Hello there! Now take a deep breath. I think I know how you feel right now. You are either feeling not good enough, stressed, fearful, uptight, overwhelmed, or unhappy. You may be feeling all of these emotions. Some of you may know what you want (even though you may not yet have it) and others may still feel unsure about what you truly desire. But either way, you are most likely overwhelmed trying to figure out how to feel peace, confidence and happiness. You've tried to make changes and failed so many times that you almost believe change isn't really possible for you and true happiness is out of your reach.

This book is an invitation to just be still and stop striving to be perfect, to be someone you are not. Throughout the book, I will assist you in releasing the negative beliefs you have about yourself, because of the high expectations you have set for yourself. You'll learn processes to allow you to let go of your struggles and your fears and to let go of your insecurities and the feelings of "not being good enough".

We are creators. We were destined to create more than you may currently imagine is possible. You were created for a purpose. You were created to shine bright. It's time to be free. Free of shame, guilt, fear and to be free to fully live!

Sister, don't wait to live. Start now! You don't need to be 'ready' to create the life you want. Don't do what I did and say "when XYZ happens… then I'll be ready to change". The truth is that XYZ never happens (and if it does, you've lost years of happiness waiting). If you fall into this trap, your commitment to change will be put off for no reason. You will have delayed feeling excited for each new day and 'sexy confident' because of a lie!

The enemy of taking action is the false belief in "someday". That is a day which never arrives. We tend to think our life will eventually overtake our dreams and then we'll suddenly be living this magical life we hoped for, but never planned for. Sounds ridiculous to expect that to happen, right? Yet too many of us think the happy future of our dreams will happen without a plan and without taking action today.

We all have a list of "someday I'll…" that keeps growing.

What are you waiting for? Permission? Acceptance? Approval?

I invite you to decide now that you will take action today on what you learn in this book. Decide to seek help, where needed, in creating habits and change. If by now you haven't overcome the procrastination to take action towards your dreams on your own, it's unlikely this time will be any different, unless you now choose to do something different.

I don't say that to discourage you, I say that to encourage you to try a different approach. Find support. Find a "community" of like minded people to help you create the change that leads to your dream body, relationship, and life.

Don't wait for me to say go. Don't wait for the right words or best plan or perfect time. Just start where you are. Let's get started!

# CHAPTER 1

# WHAT IS MINDSTRENGTH?

# WHAT IS MINDSTRENGTH?

The best way to clearly explain MindStrength, is to start by sharing the story of how I identified the MindStrength Process.

Throughout the first 12 years of my marriage, I was on a wave cycle when it came to working out. I would work out a total of 3 to 4 months in a year. I'd start working out, feel like I was committed and motivated, but then after about 30-45 days I'd lose motivation because I didn't believe I was seeing the results that 30-45 days of exercise should have produced, then I'd give up. This cycle was 1 to 2 months of working out and then 3 to 5 months of nothing.

I was so focused on being motivated by seeing results that I stopped exercising, even though I felt good when I did exercise consistently.

Finally, in 2013 I decided to do something different. I began to go to a gym where I felt like I was part of a community of like minded, non-judgmental people. I made a small commitment at that time. My commitment wasn't to be perfect with the exercises I was learning and certainly not in regards to nutrition either. I wasn't eating the right foods or even the right amount of calories, but I showed up and exercised anyway. I wasn't focused on seeing any physical change this time around.

My commitment was simply to go to the gym 3 days a week at 8:00AM for a group class doing bodyweight training using TRX suspension trainers. I admit, after a while I was going almost just for the social aspect. Some of the women in that 8:00AM class became my friends and cheerleaders and kept me wanting to come back.

Over time, that commitment became easy, so I increased my commitment to 5 days a week. Soon, that became easy too and I then started going at 5:00AM for 5 days a week.

After a few months I began to go from just doing a body weight workout class with the TRX suspension trainer to almost exclusively working out with kettlebells.

I didn't really feel like I was very strong when I started working out with kettlebells. My coaches and trainers at the gym kept encouraging me as they were seeing the improvements I was making. I was relying a lot on the faith and belief my coaches had in me. I didn't really believe I was strong and capable of hard things at the time.

This is where I began to recognize changes in my mind that allowed me to begin to make other changes outside of "going to the gym 5 times a week".

As I worked out using heavier weights, I would notice that my confidence in the gym was soaring. Not because I was the strongest, but because I was getting stronger than I was before.

Then one of my coaches randomly asked me if I would consider becoming a certified kettlebell trainer. I was instantly scared by the thought. I hadn't really thought outside of my default roles of a wife and a mother. After I let the initial shock sink in, I decided to do something uncomfortable which I never before would have considered to be capable of doing. I decided to train to become a certified kettlebell instructor.

The coach that challenged me to do this, Rob Morris (a tough guy who I saw as someone who can do hard things - after all, he played in the NFL for 8 years and won a Super Bowl playing for the Colts) was my constant motivator from that point on. He was the one who said over and over again to me that it was possible for me to do this thing which I perceived to be hard. He saw something in me that I didn't see in myself at the time. He was my biggest cheerleader (I can imagine Rob dressed like a cheerleader, because I've seen his Halloween outfits... if you text ROB to 877-858-1510, I'll send you the photo that pops into my mind).

I felt challenged and it felt so good to push my body to do hard things and prepare for the challenge of passing off the physical aspects of this certification.

This led to the day that I discovered what I call MindStrength. It happened in San Diego, California at my three day StrongFirst Kettlebell Instructor Certification Course.

While I was there over the course of three days, I kept telling myself, "I can do this. I've worked hard to get here. I can make this happen".

It was very hard at times, but I tried to stay positive in my thoughts and numb the pain. The more I fought, the more overwhelming it became. The tension came in waves with short releases between, but not enough time to renew my strength, only enough time to have negative thoughts creep in and doubt my ability to get through it.

By this time I had been participating in intense kettlebell training for 8 hours a day and almost 2.5 days straight. My hands were blistered and in pain. Doubt turned to desperation. "Why am I so weak? I can't keep up with those in my group. Who am I to be here? What makes me think I can be among all of these strong and athletic personal trainers? I'm just a mom with 4 children!"

I feared the unknown, compared myself with others, and feared not being in full control. Until that moment, that had been my experience. I pleaded with God for help in the middle of this intense physical experience. I knew that if I just let go of my negative self talk, stopped comparing with others and released any expectations to control my outcome, that my experience would change.

After I had prayed I realized that there was no way out of this experience but to get through and finish as best I could and accept the outcome, whatever it may be.

I began to feel my confidence build up as I looked back on my preparation and recognized all those who were supporting me. My husband had faith in me and had taken time away from work to be with the children and had allowed me to invest in myself so I could do this. My coach Rob was there with me and was encouraging me to stay strong and told me I could do this hard thing.

I decided to no longer dwell on those negative thoughts and focused instead on the belief that I was capable of doing hard things and that my preparation was sufficient to get me through. I chose to think instead, "I'm going to pass my strength and written tests and become a certified kettlebell instructor!"

The final day of my 3 day kettlebell certification course is the day I learned this life-altering truth:

**My need for control and perfection was holding me back in all areas of my life. My new life would come not only by my own might, but through surrendering control and accepting imperfection while I put forth my best effort.**

I believe the self confidence I had developed in 2013 as I focused on one commitment - to work out consistently - was the biggest contributor to my success and allowed me to get through those 3 days in San Diego.

As soon as I recognized what I had accomplished my confidence was at an all time high and I thought to myself, "What else is possible for me to do?" This confidence started spilling over into other areas of my life. Because my family is my highest priority, I soon started to seek more information on

Rob Morris & I at the StrongFirst Certification, San Diego, Feb 2014

how to improve my communication and relationships with my husband and my children.

As my confidence increased with my relationships with my husband and children I thought about how else I could create happiness and success in other areas of my life. Soon, friends and family began to notice a change in me.

This is MindStrength!

MindStrength is the process of creating confidence in one area of your life, first where you are most likely to succeed, and then taking that strength and confidence and leveraging it to build confidence in other areas of your life.

We do this by first making a small commitment, then follow simple daily practices and processes to create a genuine belief in our ability to stay committed. We take action on the things which will help solidify this new positive belief until that new action or commitment becomes easy and our confidence soars in that area of our life. We can then use this new found confidence and choose another area of our life to improve. Rinse and repeat.

In Chapter 9 I'll share some real life examples of how the MindStrength process works and in Chapter 11 I'll share the secret to actually creating change that lasts. These simple mental and physical processes along with confidence creating habits will assist you in uncovering your inner strength and finding the REAL POWERFUL YOU, who will then easily be able to create the life, body and relationships that you want!

In spite of my flaws, weaknesses and the frequent mistakes that I make, people have been drawn to me because of my confidence. The reason so many women who have known me have recently approached me and asked me to mentor them is because they saw the "before and after" not only of my body, but of my confidence and how I now carry myself.

I don't see myself as better than anyone, but I can now see myself as God sees me and that level of confidence is what we all desire.

As women have approached me, they can't put into words what made them feel drawn to talk to me. But once I explain the MindStrength process and how we get to create success one step at a time and that confidence is the natural byproduct of this process, they tell me that's exactly what they desire.

After about a year into using the MindStrength process, my husband Trent told me that I had "sexy confidence". As you can imagine I just laughed it off, but he further explained what he meant by that. He said, *"The more and more confident you've become over the last year, the more sexy you are to me. It's not even the changes in your body, but the changes in you and how you carry yourself. Your confidence is so attractive and makes me want to be even closer to you. You're sexy confident."*

I believe when your mind, body and spirit are aligned in working towards your purpose you embody "sexy confidence".

In the past when I would hear the word "sexy" I would react in a negative way because of the meaning I had given that word. It was a dirty word to me. If my husband told me I was sexy, I would immediately feel naughty and dirty.

Recently, I began to understand that the definition of "sexy" isn't just about sex. "Sexy" is not just having beautiful lips, a perfect face, nice hair, or a nice body. Sexy goes beyond that. To me, "sexy" is the confident energy a person produces that attracts others. "Sexy" is the comfortable feeling of being who you are. It's about a person who embodies connection, attraction and growth.

When you have sexy confidence, people who meet you admire your sense of self-esteem and feel attracted to you. Not necessarily in a sexual way, but in a curious way. When you walk into a room, people notice you because you hold your head up high and stand up tall. Not because of pride, but because you are confident and not concerned with what others might think about you. You don't dwell on doubt, judgment from others or uncertainty long enough to get you down and that is truly "sexy".

Through the MindStrength Process you will grow from fear of judgment, fear of failure, and fear of change until you can, on your own, create the life you choose.

You may feel stress and anxiety as we discuss the causes and symptoms of this prevalent problem of not feeling good enough. However, I promise that I will share some solutions that worked for me and others and how you can start on the path to developing MindStrength and become "sexy confident".

The truth is that you are stronger than you believe. Physically, emotionally, and mentally.

*"Birth is not only about making babies. Birth is about making mothers - strong, competent, capable mothers who trust themselves and know their inner strength."*

-Barbara Katz Rothman

## CHAPTER 2

# CHASING
# PERFECTION

# CHASING PERFECTION

*"God knows that you are not perfect. As you suffer about your imperfections, he will give you comfort and suggestions of where to improve."*

-F. Enzio Busche

You know that feeling you get when a good friend asks, "How are you?" and you instantly tense up, not wanting to reveal the stuff that's really weighing you down?

You think to yourself, "I can't tell her. It's too much. I wont be able to stop if I start. I might start crying. I don't want to burden her. She will think I'm crazy."

If we try to appear as though we are "perfect" in spite of all the troubles we are dealing with in our mind, we may respond to this question with, "I'm good". We all seem to say those two words when asked how we are doing without taking any thought. What would happen if we actually opened up and said more than those two perfect words?

Do you feel like you are chasing perfection in some ways? Are attempting to measure up to an external standard? Do you put on the "I'm doing good" face to the rest of the world?

You don't need to pretend that your life is perfect. I am not saying you're not perfect as you are, but your life definitely is not perfect! No one's is!

Life, our peers, our family and everyday experiences have probably convinced you that you are far from perfect. We too often attach our mistakes and experiences to our own self worth and feel that because our life isn't perfect, we aren't perfect and therefore, we must not be good enough.

I was doing what I thought I was supposed to do to be a good mom, wife and woman. Raise righteous children, have a sparkling clean home, drive the nicest car, wear the latest fashions and be put together every day, plus have an incredible marriage and let's be honest, I wanted to live like June Cleaver from the 50's.

I feared for the longest time that if I slowed down I would no longer be productive. I feared my life would be meaningless if I wasn't perfectly fulfilling my duties as well as striving for something bigger and better. It was exhausting!

What I experienced, that frequently reminded me that I was not good enough, was seeing other moms taking their kids on adventures, creating elaborate birthday parties and presenting their children all crisp and clean cut in the latest fashion trends. This list of things that made me not feel good enough as a mom could go on for pages.

I eventually bought into this idea that I needed to be doing more in order to be the "perfect mom". Then day after day, year after year my heartache grew and I felt I didn't know how to do it all and keep my life together. I became numb and just followed the crowd and didn't take one thought of how it was affecting me inside.

What are we trying to prove when we live this way? What are we doing to ourselves? What's the one thing we are racing towards?

For me it was to be "perfect" so I could return to live forever in peace with God.

This chase for perfection disguises itself in lists of "should's".

"I should work out every day."
"I should eat healthy."
"I should spend more time playing with my kids."
"I should work hard now so I can enjoy my life later."
"I should or I won't be enough."
"I should do this or that."
"I should live this way."

I have since replaced "I should..." with "I'm going to". For example when I say, "I should go spend one on one time with Reeghan" it feels forced and not heartfelt. But when I say, "I am going to spend one on one time with Reeghan." I am making a choice, not expressing a feeling of forced obligation. It is something I enjoy and choose to do.

Our words we speak out into the world start in our minds and when we use the words, "should, have to, try, etc" they are words that stand still. They have no movement. What would happen if we removed those words from our vocabulary? Who says you have to live by those rules? What if ending the chase means intentionally leaning in to what might feel imperfect?

What would your life look like if you took out the "should's, have to's and try's"? Maybe our house won't be spick and span, maybe our work project wasn't as crisp as we would have liked, maybe our child's outfit didn't quite coordinate together? But your kids will feel loved, and you will have time with your husband or friend because you chose to slow down and take time to listen and to show up imperfect.

We read in the scriptures, "Be ye therefore perfect" and in my mind it meant that I had to live up to a certain standard and make no mistakes if I wanted to live with my Father in Heaven. The more life experience I have, the more I understand what this scripture really means. It teaches me to strive each day to live like Christ and accept that only through Christ can I be perfected. I, Sarah Chapman, cannot be perfect on my own, but I had believed that is what God was telling me.

For so long I believed I had to be a perfect wife, mother, and daughter. I thought I had to be obedient and perfect in ALL things. My belief was that if I wasn't perfect, then I wasn't good enough, not loveable and I wouldn't be "acceptable" to God. My lie was "If I'm not perfect, I'm not loveable".

Over time the impossible standards I set up for myself became a measuring stick for my worth. I started to believe that if I didn't measure up to all the standards set by others, I wasn't enough. I began to feel worthless.

I was fueled by quick fixes that didn't fix anything at all. I believed the lies about who I was and wasn't supposed to be. I chased the standard of 'perfect'.

Chasing perfect makes us believe we are average or even insignificant.

Chasing perfect makes us believe we will never be content.

Chasing perfect makes us believe we don't have enough friends, enough happiness, enough fun or enough adventures.

Chasing perfect is often revealed when we are comparing our worth with someone else's.

Chasing perfect makes us believe we aren't good moms, wives, and friends.

Chasing perfect makes us do unreasonable things, like starving ourselves, and buying things we don't really want and can't really afford, to measure up to others' expectations.

What has chasing perfect and striving for impossible standards made you believe?

Perfection is out of your reach in this life. The pursuit of perfection has created several other sad beliefs about our worth and destroys the confidence of millions and millions of people. In the next chapter we will dive deeper into why this belief in "being perfect" separates us from the peace and happiness we seek.

# CHAPTER 3

# NOT GOOD ENOUGH

# NOT GOOD ENOUGH

Do you ever feel like "I'm not good enough"?

Do you ever judge yourself and think, "I'm a screw up" when you make a mistake?

If you don't meet other people's expectations, do you feel that you're not good enough?

Do you procrastinate a lot?

Are you worried that what you are putting off doing won't be good enough when you finally do it?

Even beyond dealing with the idea of "being perfect", we all have experiences in our lives that present to our minds this idea that we aren't good enough in one way or another.

I sure struggled with the thought that I wasn't smart enough or that I didn't know enough. As a teenager, I remember being in a class in high school and being called on to explain something I didn't understand. The words wouldn't come and I felt like I was babbling. I was embarrassed and started to think, "I guess I don't really know that much".

That nasty lie and confidence destroying thought was not intentionally placed there by any one person. It was accepted by my mind because of my naive interpretation of that experience. That one thought and experience had held me down for years.

Because I believed I didn't know enough, in my marriage I would never speak my mind, even when I had something important to share, because I feared I didn't know enough and wouldn't be able to speak my mind clearly. So what did I do instead? I bottled things up inside. This one negative thought, interpreted from one experience as a teenager, began to be the basis of many problems I created in my life.

What interpretation of a childhood experience has created false beliefs about yourself?

If it isn't bad enough that we misinterpret childhood experiences, we are constantly bombarded by the media telling us that in order to be acceptable or good enough, we need to look, act and speak a certain way.

It's impossible to live up to these expectations and most of us get to the point where we throw our hands up in the air and just give up because we can't keep up. We start to feel depressed and this downward spiral gets worse.

While I was finishing writing this book, I asked hundreds of women to participate in a questionnaire with the promise that I would keep them anonymous as they shared their answers. One of the questions I asked was:

"What are some of the messages from outside influences that you hear/see, suggesting that you have to "be" a certain way to be "ok" or "good enough"?

Here are the answers from a couple of women:

*"I think for many of us, we have to be skinny, fashionable, have a cute house and perfectly put together family to be good enough. On social media people only post the "pretty" stuff, not the everyday and we often feel like we're falling short."*

*"Magazines, websites, books, movies, music, actors, toys (Barbies), video games, clothing and clothing sizes. I've never watched these shows, but the "Real Housewives" reality shows, basically only have women who are wealthy, obsessed with being sickly thin, perfectly put together in every way and pay for help. That is a perfect example. The size of our homes now is 3x larger than they were in the 40's and 50's. Our society as a whole pressures us to fit into an "ideal" which isn't healthy. Yet because I'm not an "average" person, I'm the odd one out, in all aspects of my life. It royally sucks."*

What is the ideal? Who says we have to conform to the ideal? We know that most magazine covers have airbrushed models touched up by people with amazing photoshop skills. You also read crazy promises on the covers such as, "Get your booty back in 30 days!" As a society is this where we are getting our health and fitness education from? Pure false expectations!

Another woman responded to my question with this answer:

*"I struggle so much with body image. My head tells me that women that are anything like me pay good money to "fix" their looks, which I internalize as, "I am gross or undesirable". Most women I associate with have plastic surgery, and I question if I have worth without doing that to my body. Am I enough if I am or am not a certain size, style, etc?"*

Recently in the media we've been hearing the right message that you need to love yourself, but they don't share 'how' to love yourself. If it was as easy as just deciding, I think we would have a much more confident and secure society as a whole. So many women have told me, "How am I supposed to love myself when I look in the mirror and see a fat slob?".

There is a process to loving yourself which I will share in Chapter 5. The results of following this process are not immediate, but over time, it will allow you to see yourself through God's eyes and not the World's. You'll start to compare yourself with the previous version of you as you improve instead of comparing yourself with other people! Sounds like a dream to many women to finally not feel judged and not good enough, but it's not a dream, it can be your reality.

We accept standards or beliefs outside of ourselves and we start to believe the messages we hear out in the world. We misinterpret God's message of "be ye therefore perfect", which makes us feel like failures when we aren't perfect. Perfectionism is the misunderstood path to feeling like a failure and forgetting we are His daughters on a path that is full of mistakes and wrong turns. Mistakes are expected from all of us, not perfection in this moment!

The perfection cycle continues daily if we don't choose to stop the cycle ourselves and go to the root cause of why we feel emptiness in the first place. This is where The MindStrength 5 Step Process assists you in becoming aware and asking yourself the right questions to get you out of the cycle. In chapter 9 I'll share this amazing process and how it's helped other women.

# CHAPTER 4

# STUMBLING BLOCKS TO CONNECTION

# STUMBLING BLOCKS TO CONNECTION

I remember many times in my life where I seemed to have judged every person, man or woman on my left and my right and of course myself! I was out to judge everyone. I was in a constant thought process of judgment. Seeing them in a way that was not as God saw them.

At that point in my life I had very low self worth and was not sexy confident. I wanted to look to others and judge them as if they had less worth than I. I'd look for ways to find the negative in them to help me feel better about where I was.

It was a very dark time in my life. I had never sunk so deep and I sure wasn't raised to think these thoughts about others. One particular period in my life I had just had my first baby and had added 40 pounds on my already 155 pound body. I didn't know what I was doing. I kept looking at others to see how to do things and try to figure things out, but I would just continue to beat myself up because I was once again "not good enough" to do this mom thing along with taking care of myself.

I started to compare myself as a mother to my mother-in-law and sisters-in-law who had children at the time I became a mother. I just remember the weight I felt to live up to where they were. I felt as though I was being judged all day long and I never wanted to make a mistake in front of them.

Whenever I was around them I fought to prove to them that I was doing an okay job as a mother. I remember using that word "fight" and thinking to myself about the definition that I created for that word. Fight meant to me to prove, to show up competitively (which isn't my nature to be competitive) and to walk into situations as a mother with two clinched hands up by my face, ready to protect myself.

Comparison and judgement are so prevalent. We compare our failures with everyone's successes. By their nature, comparison and judgment force a single winner. One gets to be thinner, stronger, prettier, smarter, younger, cuter, or better.

In what area of your life do you see this the most? Within your family, on social media, at the gym, your children's school or even at church?

When it comes to following other women in social media I want you to ask yourself: Is this woman making me feel better about ME?

Too often I see women on social media post comments such as these on photos of seemingly flawless bodies:

"I wish I looked like her"
"I want my body to look like that"
"Why can't I be her?"
"Why can't I have that life?"
"Why can't I be perfect like you?"

Creating an illusion like you have a perfect life and a perfect body is dishonest. It's not actually helping as many people as it's hurting. And wishing for someone else's life or body isn't going to help you live a vibrant, healthy life you were meant to live.

I've fallen into this trap myself and I walk away feeling less than others. I grew tired of feeling like the measuring stick of my self worth came from the things I saw in social media. So once again I ask, "Do they make you feel good about YOU or do they make you wish that you had what they have?

In the past I felt an increase in comparison and judgement as a mother when I would go to a neighborhood park with my children or a setting with a lot of other parents and children. I didn't want to parent in front of others, especially if my child was the cause of a scene. It created a lot of anxiety and I dreaded going outside of the home with my children. Some days I would get sick to my stomach thinking about it.

Another place where I felt compared and judged was at church. I felt a lot of pressure to appear flawless when I would enter church, where my family is expected to maintain reverence as we are worshipping God.

I would walk into church and immediately think everyone was looking at me. I had no self confidence and my mind immediately turned to worrying about how others might be judging me by how I looked, answered questions, or by how my children acted. I would hardly make any comments in classes at church and I would avoid being the center of attention.

Because of these false beliefs about who we should be, how we should look, how much we should do, we fall into a state of constant judgment.

We've judged ourselves so much that we then fear judgement of our spouse or other people in our life. How many of us are driven by fear? Fear of being unhappy the rest of our life. Fear of failure. Fear of not knowing enough. Fear of disappointing someone you love. Fear of not being loved.

Fear kills dreams. Fear kills hope. Fear of what may happen, also known as worry or anxiety, creates a false reality where we feel threatened even if nothing bad has actually happened. Many times when I had felt fear and anxiety, I desired to change. I feared that making a change would worsen the situation and make me feel stuck.

Fear isn't a thing. We can't touch it, pick it up or remove it. It can't be crushed, ignored or buried either.

*"Avoid any fear like your worst enemy"*

-F. Enzio Busche

I feared that my husband Trent wouldn't love me as much if he knew the true, imperfect me. I truly had this fear and over the first 12 years of our marriage I wouldn't engage in meaningful heartfelt conversations because I wanted to keep my wall up. This lead to unauthentic communication.

Then, because of my belief that I didn't know enough, I feared that Trent would think I'm not smart and capable. This would lead to me shutting down all communication.

You'll see an example of this scenario in Chapter 9 where I talk about how I changed the old pattern of communication and correcting the negative thought: "I am not smart enough".

I felt like I was not an equal to my husband whenever he tried to talk about difficult things. I felt walked all over because of the words that he shared with me triggered me into thinking I didn't know enough. I would then of course shut down, not share my own thoughts and just let it go. I would try to sweep it under the rug as if nothing ever happened.

On the inside this belief that I was not good enough grew and grew because I chose not to deal with things and communicate how I was really feeling. Trent had no intention of making me feel this way. When I finally addressed this in 2013, it brought him to tears to think how I interpreted his desire to communicate with me as him judging me as not smart enough and not an equal partner with him.

This lack of authentic communication not only happened in my marriage, but it also happened with my other relationships. I would just let people walk all over me and take advantage of me because I didn't want to communicate my own feelings and I would just tell myself to get over it.

Deep down we each have a desire to be loved. Unfortunately this desire causes us to do things in a way that actually impedes our opportunity to experience more love. When I believed "I am not good enough" or "I don't know enough", I would hide my true self from those I loved.

I pretended to be as everyone wanted me to be, because I thought that in order to be accepted and loved I had to meet others expectations.

I also noticed when I felt this way that I gave the impression to Trent that he wasn't good enough either. I would put him down about the things he wasn't doing for our family. At one point in our marriage it was so bad that we were talking through emails instead of face to face. We didn't know how to communicate and one or the other would have to walk away to avoid getting into an argument.

Poor communication results in poor relationships. We all know this and we hear it time and time again. When we are feeling judged, we forget how to react appropriately because we are so conditioned to react defensively when attacked or judged.

When one partner isn't authentic in their communication, then neither tend to be authentic. If one is holding back, the other doesn't feel secure in being fully exposed and fully authentic. It is way easier for most people to be completely naked physically in front of their spouse than it is to be fully exposed, mentally and emotionally through their words.

The source of most of my struggles in marriage was because of our poor communication.

Poor communication meant that we didn't talk about sex either.

I grew up in a household where sex wasn't talked about at all. Growing up in a religious home, all I would hear about sex was that I shouldn't do it, that only bad girls did it and I would be dirty if I did. I did also hear "wait until you're married", but that was the extent of what I knew about sex from my family.

Did anyone else grow up this way? I'm sure I am not alone in this.

I would hear in church how God ordained sex as a sacred way to connect between a man and a woman, but that's all I seemed to hear. It was one of those hush hush topics. Luckily (or unfortunately) I had a friend who exposed me to some information about it before I got married, otherwise I think I would have been completely naive as to the mechanics of sex.

Now I don't mean for it to sound like I felt my parents didn't teach me correctly it's simply because they didn't talk about sex openly. They just chose not to expose us to the topic with a hope that we'd figure it out when we were old enough. I believe it was taboo to talk about sex in the culture I was raised in, which made it harder for my parents than it is for parents today.

So you can imagine what my wedding night was like. I just felt "thrown into it" not knowing what to expect and not understanding how to connect sexually. I chose to accept sex as naughty and although I enjoyed it, I thought of it that way each time we had sex.

For the better part of 12 years of my marriage sex wasn't a topic spoken of frequently. If Trent wanted to talk about it, I would shut him down and avoid it. Most often this would come up at night when the kids were in bed and I'd just roll over and pretend I was asleep. I know that sounds weird, especially when you're married to someone, but that was the reality of my situation. We had never really spoken about it openly and our sex life just coasted along.

Sex felt like a chore to me and a "have to" on my checklist of keeping my relationship alive on most occasions. I saw it as, "pleasure for him". Sex was an act that I didn't feel connected to in my own body, because I despised it. I had thought so many negative things about it.

When I look back, my lack of communication and fear of authenticity were because of two things. I didn't love myself and I feared that Trent might not love me if he knew I wasn't perfect! It's such a ridiculous thought, but it kept me stuck for years!

Because I didn't love myself, I couldn't let others make the mistake of fully loving me either! I pushed people away from me. I wanted to stay hidden from others because I just couldn't push myself to the next level on the measuring stick of perfection. I chased perfection so much that it lead me down a path of not loving myself.

## CHAPTER 5

# LOOK TO THE ONE WHO CREATED YOU

# LOOK TO THE ONE WHO CREATED YOU

I was the type of person who would be consistent at exercising for one or two months then take a three to five month break from my health and nutrition goals. Each time this happened, I would feel confused as to why I had given up after being so committed and excited in the beginning.

The last two years I've learned that the problem wasn't the diet or the program. It was my self worth. I would get motivated, get excited, change my diet, start a new exercise program, get new exercise clothes (They are so comfy, aren't they?) and then a few weeks later, I'd become frustrated because I wasn't seeing the miraculous transformation I expected (you know, because of all the incredible before and after photos of the "program of the month" I'd chosen).

Like most people, I believed if I would just get the attractive body... THEN I'd love myself. If I could just use my willpower consistently for a few months and be strict with my exercise and diet plan, THEN I'd be happy with myself!

Sadly, it isn't that easy and that's not the way things work. Until we love ourselves deeply and are authentic with who we are, it's almost impossible to be consistent with those things that will actually change our bodies and create the total mind and body transformation that we are seeking.

So, how do I love myself, in spite of starting out feeling like a fat slob?!?

Here is what finally worked for me and has worked for my clients. It's one of the greatest tools I've tested for expressing love to myself each morning. It has changed me to now fully believe that I have accepted myself as I am right now on my path to becoming a better version of myself.

This daily practice I'm about to share is the hardest step for most women to practice each day. It takes weeks or months for these beliefs to even take hold in their heart and mind, but yet this process is the catalyst for change.

Learning how to TRULY love yourself as you are, while you learn the tools to carry you on to be who you want to be actually happens when you follow this daily practice. I've seen it work through my own experience as well as through the experiences of other women that I've coached through this process.

Some of you reading this currently may not even like looking at yourself in the mirror and don't enjoy what you see on the outside. You may be judging yourself every time you look in the mirror, which is what makes this first daily practice so difficult for most women.

This is a process I have named, "Love Yourself from the Inside Out". It's also one part of a process I was taught by some of my mentors which allowed me to personally gain my self confidence and realize that I am enough as I am right now.

## "LOVE YOURSELF FROM THE INSIDE OUT"

Spending a couple minutes in front of a mirror everyday working on yourself makes a big difference in your attitude and well-being. Give yourself the time each day to do this exercise either in the morning or a night or both.

Stand in front of a mirror (full length is best, but any will do) standing in the "Wonder Woman" pose (hands on your hips, shoulders back, chin up slightly) and take a few deep breaths. See yourself as if you were looking through the eyes of God vs. your own judgment. You are his precious daughter. You are a queen.

State what you are great at right now, today. This can be something small to start.

Acknowledge the successes of the week or day so far.

Speak the new beliefs you are focusing on.

Speak gratitude to yourself.

Repeat this every day.

## FREE RESOURCE:

If you would like the detailed explanation of the "Love Yourself From the Inside Out" exercise along with more examples of how to perform the exercise, text the word **INSIDE** to (877) 858-1510 and I'll send you a download link for the .pdf file to view on your smartphone or computer.

It may sound silly for some and overly simplistic for others, but this may be the only chance you have to speak love to yourself, out loud. You will also get to focus on your own needs without the distractions of your responsibilities for others.

Wake up early if you need to, but absolutely make time to prioritize your health and happiness first. I do this every day after I shower! My children have also started doing this exercise everyday too as Trent or I drive them to school. It's already begun to affect our children in a positive way.

This exercise was one of many habits that I've implemented in my life that has contributed to my process in creating MindStrength. I set myself up each morning with power to handle whatever would come to me that day good or bad. A proper attitude towards growth can be developed and improved, it just takes some patience and time.

As I continually did this exercise each day, I began to notice the confidence in my voice. At the beginning I had a hard time believing the words I was speaking. This exercise allowed me to put me first in the morning and not just jump into helping others. It was a time to reflect and think about who I was and what I wanted to become.

I began to hear and see my body language change each morning and I started to love myself through God's eyes. I was finally able to recognize and see myself as if I was looking through the eyes of God versus my own perception and judgment.

The best way I knew for me to find out about ME was to go to the source of who created ME. When I sought to be aligned with God and saw my weaknesses as things to work out with Him instead of on my own, my life became easier.

I felt so humbled and broken and in need of Him. I had reached a point where I threw up my hands and said to Him, "save me"! I handed over all my negative thoughts and beliefs that I had about myself in order to learn how to LOVE myself as I am right now. When I began to approach God in this way, I connected with Him on such a deep level.

I heard a talk by Dieter F. Uchtdorf that perfectly illustrated this experience I had of feeling not good enough. He shares how you go from this dark place to then becoming enlightened to who you are as a daughter of God in a way that I could no longer judge myself as not good enough. I am His daughter. I am a Queen. He who is perfect and who created me loves me as I am right now, so who am I NOT to love myself as I am right now.

Enlightenment means the full comprehension of a situation. Bringing understanding, clarity, wisdom, awareness and insight into a reality you were not aware of.

In this talk, Dieter spoke of a picture that hangs in his office titled, "Entrance to Enlightenment", which shows the doorway to a room and most of the room is darkened. The doorway has a sliver of light in the entrance.

He spoke of this painting as a metaphor about life. He talked about how we may only see what's in front of us most of the time because we have been filled with so much darkness most of our life. This darkness comes from our trials and the negative thoughts on which we dwell. It comes from feeling like I'm "fat", "not pretty", "not a good mom", "not smart enough" and thousands of other false thoughts. It can come from doubts and fears about who we are, worrying about what could happen, or even feeling completely alone and not loved.

The point is, it's okay to recognize that darkness does exist and how real and relevant it is, but instead of focusing on the darkness and linger there, allow yourself to see the real YOU through God's eyes. You've probably heard it before, "God doesn't create junk". This daily process will enlighten you so you can see who you truly are and accept your divinity as a daughter of God.

*"For the word of the Lord is truth, and whatsoever is truth is light, and whatsoever is light is Spirit, even the Spirit of Jesus Christ. And the Spirit giveth light to every man that cometh into the world; and the Spirit enlighteneth every man through the world, that hearkeneth to the voice of the Spirit."*
-Doctrine & Covenants 84:45-46

# CHAPTER 6

# SEXY CONFIDENCE

# SEXY CONFIDENCE

Ultimately what you think of YOU is what has the most impact on who you are and how you act or react. For this reason, before I focus on teaching women about exercise or eating habits, I focus all of my time, energy and effort on cleaning up the mind.

Thinking, but more importantly, believing that you are someone capable and worthy of good things is what sets positive change into motion. By following simple daily practices your heart begins to change. You will begin to see, think, feel and believe that your life can be really good and that you are worthy of the dreams that you may have let go of. No, this is not some fairy tale, but until you experience this change for yourself, it may seem like one.

What does it take to jumpstart you back on the path to believing that you can create the life, body and relationships you want? How do you get to the point where you believe that you actually deserve the life you have dreamed of?

I've identified four parts of my path to confidence that allowed me to change my mind, body and relationships. Each of these four things can work wonders in creating change, but together they will cause you to experience transformational change.

# PART 1 - DECIDE WHAT YOU REALLY WANT AND SET GOALS.

For most people, deciding what they want in life is not very easy to describe, if they know at all. Others have a clear picture and a path to follow. The first step for me in creating the life I wanted was deciding, "What do I really want?"

That is such a simple question, but it has tremendous power! When you clearly identify what you want your body, life and relationships to look like, God begins to prepare your path.

Don't fall into the trap of thinking that the worlds "standards and expectations" are the same as your own "wants".

When I started working out consistently, I had to ask myself, "Do I really want the 'bikini body' that the world tells women that we should have or am I happy to have a healthy body that allows me to move and enjoy life experiences with my family?"

There isn't one answer that is right for everyone. The answer for you and in each area of your life may be very different from mine. I had to decide what I wanted and ignore what I thought I was "supposed" to want because of outside standards and influences. This is the important part. Truly analyze what you "want" and make sure it isn't what the World is telling you that you should want.

In my relationship with my husband, I asked myself a similar question, "What do I want my relationship with my husband to look like?"

When I decided that I really wanted a close, meaningful and authentic relationship with my husband, it allowed me to believe that I could create a better marriage than the one I was living. I have to say, back when I first started asking myself "what do I want", I didn't know that my relationship could become as deep and authentic as it is today.

You can do this process of asking, "What do I really want?" and apply it to any area of your life. These are the 5 areas I generally focus on:

1. Mental (learning & mental growth)

2. Spiritual (becoming one with God)

3. Emotional (relationship with spouse, children & loved ones)

4. Physical (my body, health, energy & physical achievements)

5. Financial (income and wealth)

## PART 2 - IDENTIFY DAILY PRACTICES TO SUPPORT YOU IN CREATING THE BELIEF.

This step is all about the mind and spirit. These are not healthy body habits, but healthy habits for the mind and soul. I discovered that to have the body, life and relationships that I wanted, I would need to grow mentally and spiritually to overcome the negative thoughts and beliefs that had held me back. I knew that I would benefit from following daily practices and a process for creating change.

When I started on this path to MindStrength, in order to truly love myself and approve of who I was (while I worked at becoming a better version of me), I started doing the "Love Yourself from the Inside Out" exercise from the previous chapter.

As I saw progress in my health and accepting and loving myself, I was motivated to do more and added to my daily process. I added daily personal scripture study, prayer, meditation and finished with a brief visualization of what I wanted to create that day.

I now do this every morning and it is my highest priority. If this morning ritual is the only thing I do all day to appreciate and love myself, I am okay with that. I have to admit though, it wasn't easy at first to do these things and I still struggle some days, but I know the power it gives me if it is done each morning.

This allows me to see myself through God's eyes and to love all of my imperfect self. As I repeated this process the first few weeks, my subconscious mind kept reminding me of all my shortcomings and I would feel that I was just lying to myself. Then things started to change. After about a month of this daily routine, I noticed something amazing.

I noticed as I went through this routine that I did love and accept myself. All 100% of the imperfect Sarah. I acknowledge my flaws and weaknesses, but no longer allowed those flaws to define me or set the value of Sarah Ann Chapman.

Going to the gym, eating healthy and all the positive habits I was forming began to come easier.

My mind was right, so it no longer was fighting the change, instead it was supporting me in creating the new life I was choosing for myself.

That is the key to lasting change. Take action, but work on daily routines to get your mind in alignment with what you really want.

I wouldn't have been able to create so many positive habits in my life in such a short time had I not implemented this daily routine. The changes came faster and easier the more I focused on my daily ritual to start my day off right.

## PART 3 - RECOGNIZE YOUR BLESSINGS AND WHAT YOU ALREADY DO WELL.

For many women I've coached, they begin this journey feeling like they are not good at anything. Their self worth has been decimated by their interpretation of life experiences and by their habitual reaction of turning to negative thoughts.

The only way I've found to muster up enough motivation and willpower to begin daily rituals to support change has been to focus on all the blessings I do have in my life (express gratitude to God) and to recognize the gifts I already have. Most likely, these gifts are not appreciated by the World's standards, but they are of much more worth than "looking hot".

Some wonderful women I know have felt they have no self worth because of their looks or because they have gone through divorce. What is sad is that many of them are some of the most loving, selfless women who are also great friends and great mothers.

By recognizing what you are good at or what traits and qualities you have developed, you will be able to slowly gain confidence in that area of your life. This is crucial if you currently feel worthless based on the world's standards. This confidence will assist you in creating new successes in other areas of your life.

You are great at something or consistent with something already and you can be proud of that. Own it!

## PART 4 - CHOOSE DAILY ACTIONS TO SUPPORT YOU IN GROWING.

What started my journey to confidence and self-love was the one thing I knew I was good at; working out 5 times a week. I would wake up and say to myself each morning at 4:45am the word "commit". I made a commitment to myself and to the gym I was going to that I would show up. As I began, my workouts weren't the best and I would often only give 60% effort, but I still woke up, showed up and moved my body.

I won't tell you much about my diet at the time, as it wasn't even something I thought about. I was proud that I was consistent at exercise and had self confidence because of that one act I did for myself every day. For building my confidence I used this one habit, one simple thing that I did 5 times a week that made me feel proud of myself. That's where I started.

You may start with something totally different and that's okay. It could be eating one healthy meal a day, serving your spouse, taking a walk. The point is to recognize something you do well and do it consistently until you start to feel good about your daily accomplishment. This isn't about being prideful or feeling better than others, but about loving yourself and honoring yourself to take care of you and creating the life you desire and deserve.

# CHAPTER 7

# ACCEPTANCE

# ACCEPTANCE

When I consistently did my morning routine and used The MindStrength 5 Step Process any time I felt judgement, fear, resentment, self doubt, or a lack of self worth, I slowly saw that my attitude and confidence were changing. I was actually happy with who I was.

I chose to allow God to walk with me on my journey to discover that my imperfect self could walk with Him and I was okay with that. I didn't judge it, it just was and thats the beauty of it.

*"Be not so much concerned about what you do, but do what you do with all your heart, might, and strength. In thoroughness is satisfaction.*

*You want to be good and to do good. That is commendable. But the greatest achievement that can be reached in our lives is to be under the complete influence of the Holy Ghost. Then he will teach us what is really good and necessary to do."*

-F. Enzio Busche

As a mother I wanted to prove to those around me that I was capable. I was more concerned with how they viewed me then how God saw me. With God's help I was able to grasp that He gave these children to me, on loan. If I approached motherhood with the right intent and with an open mind, I would do just fine.

I have finally come to believe that God is the one to please. For so many years I appeared to have the nice home, clean cut children, overly organized spaces, and living my life like someone else, but not feeling good enough.

My life is not out of a magazine. I don't go to a salon and get all pampered and I surely can't cook a gourmet meal or even sew my own clothes. Just to name a few things.

But among the many things I don't do or have there is ONE that I do have and I wouldn't trade it for anything. It is not a belief, but a KNOWLEDGE of a Father in Heaven who loves, listens, and walks with me regardless of those things. I've come to find Him ever so close to me now more than ever before because of my daily routine and processes.

My life is overflowing with incredible experiences and opportunities that are priceless because of that knowledge. I have learned to focus on the relationship that truly matters most, the one we have with GOD.

*"Never judge anyone. When you accept this, you will be freed. In the case of your own children or subordinates, where you have the responsibility to judge, help them to become their own judges."*

- F. Enzio Busche

As a mother raising children, I am a judge everyday. I am the one that they come to when they are fighting, when they are in need of help, when they need a shoulder to cry on, and when they just need someone to listen. I was taught a very powerful question to ask them when they come to me in distress, "Are you looking for blame or solution?" This gets their minds thinking. I'm putting them in position to become their own judges. To either create or be a victim.

I saw myself go from constant judgement to acceptance once I learned this simple principle of blame vs solution. I chose to see that living in constant judgement was exhausting! I had the tendency to make quick judgements about others. I wasn't accepting that they may be in a different place in their journey in life and that I am not better or worse than they are. By following a process to change my nature and choosing to see others as God's children, my life is now more peaceful and my relationships more rewarding.

Assuming the best in others is an act of kindness we can all give to one another. When we give others the benefit of the doubt and assume their actions come from good intent, then we create more peace in our life instead of more drama.

Have you ever bumped into someone you knew years ago, who you wouldn't have classified a "good person", but has since changed for the better? Life is full of little miracles, but this is perhaps the greatest miracle of all—to see people change, grow, and improve, day by day and little by little.

When I began to stop judging myself and beating myself up, I began to see those around me through God's eyes with a pure love and desire to help others become the potential I could see in them. I no longer judged them as they were, but tried to see their potential as God sees our potential.

Imagine how different life would be if we saw people not for who they are right now, but for who they could become. Think of how we might respond differently to a child if we looked past his failed and messy attempts to make something and instead saw his productive, positive future. Consider the boss, spouse, teenager, or neighbor whose occasional annoying behaviors sometimes put us at odds. What if we could see them as the better person they might become? This may be the most important way we can change—in our ability to believe in and nurture change in others because of who we know they can become.

It's not always easy to see others as they can become, and it very often takes patience and faith. Too often we give ourselves and others a reputation that defines them, which makes change difficult. People can surprise us, even inspire us, with how they can and often will change for the better.

Comparison and judgement of others will only stop when you stop judging yourself. You'll stop judging yourself once you see YOU through God's eyes and love the beautiful, imperfect you. This process isn't easy. It isn't fast, but you can do this and it is so worth it, sister!

# CHAPTER 8

# MIND CONTROL

# MIND CONTROL

The hardest part of breaking the chains of judgement, fear, control and the chase for perfection is seeing that you need help and guidance. If anyone in my family dealt with these things, they didn't appear to seek outside help. I didn't even know that was an option for me. I thought seeking outside help was for those who really had lots of trials and deep emotional scars.

*"Be still, and know that I am God..."*

-Psalms 46:10

Be still and know that God's desire for you is a life of peace. He wants you to feel free from the chase for perfection, the flaws, the mistakes. Regardless of what you've done or where you have been, you matter and He loves you. You were created for a purpose and it's time to find out what that is and to create the life that you want.

What did it take for me to jump off this path of constantly seeking "perfection" and be awakened to see the possibilities of the imperfect me?

In 2013, a couple months after Trent and I had hit rock bottom in our relationship (I'll share more about this story in Chapter 10), we attended a self development seminar called Live Big. This took place over our 12th anniversary and it literally changed the course of our marriage and lives.

At this event, I was awakened to the possibility that I could actually control and change my thoughts! Wait what? I can control my thoughts? Why was this a new concept for me?

Here I was, 32 years old, 4 children, a stay at home mom living day to day not really conscious of everything I was thinking about. I could recognize when I was having negative thoughts, because those would linger and make me feel worthless, but I didn't know how to get rid of them!

I learned from these mentors and coaches that I COULD actually change how I naturally react to thoughts and things that would come up in my day to day life. I can control my thoughts by being conscious and fully aware of when I start to feel those crappy days coming on (some of you may think that crappy days are normal… I hope that they will soon be a thing of the past for you). I am sure I had heard that it was possible to change our thoughts before, but I must have not been in a place to receive it.

I find I get that way in spiritual matters as well. I was raised in a Latter-day Saint, Christian household and was taught the basics about living a Christlike life and to live in a way that would bring out the best in me. But as I continued to learn and study I would have many "aw ha" moments and think to myself, "Why didn't I catch that years ago when I think I should have known that story or concept at a particular age."

But I believe it's all about timing! God knows when we need certain things to be brought to our attention and people to enter our lives when we need it most and to bring them to the forefront of our minds. And boy am I ever grateful for the timing with which this happened to me!

One day, Trent and I were having a lunch date while our children were in school and I asked him how I had ever believed that I didn't have control of my thoughts and emotions. How had I seriously believed that if I was sad, depressed, angry, etc that I had no control over that?

My husband, being the analytical type that he is, paused for a moment and then said something that struck me. He said, "We all grow up learning how to react to situations. We learn from our parents, siblings and peers how to react and there is also a small amount of our personal nature that plays a part in how we react to things. I guess what I'm saying is, we are reactive and unless we consciously focus on changing, we'll continue to react to situations in the same way we always have. Because of that, for most people it does "seem" like we don't have any control over our negative thoughts and how we react to things."

This is what struck me. Unless we consciously choose to create a different pattern, we will always react the way we've always reacted to negative thoughts and stressful situations.

I wanted to know that I could change my reactions to the thoughts I was thinking about, but I didn't know how. We all can recognize when we are feeling negative, but some of us have never paused to realize that we could actually stop ourselves from going into a negative reaction pattern.

I finally chose to hire a mentor that would help me learn how to change how I react to thoughts and experiences. I was awakened to see the possibilities in myself if I could reprogram my natural reaction to looking at my body in the mirror, feeling judged when I went to the park with my kids, comparing myself to other women who I would see at church.

This mentor taught me an exercise to help me get out of a funk when I noticed these negative thoughts and feelings (I'm not good enough, why am I such a failure, why can't I lose weight, how come I'm such a bad mom, etc).

This process helped me to identify what I was feeling and what caused that feeling. Then, I was taught to focus on what I really wanted out of that situation.

# CHAPTER 9

# D.I.V.E. &
# CREATE ACTION

# D.I.V.E. & CREATE ACTION

The process I mentioned in the last chapter served me at the beginning and one day, my husband and I discussed the steps and decided to create our own process that includes God in the process. This also makes more sense with my belief in God and how He sees me as His daughter. If you take nothing else from this book to implement, I hope you will implement this process. This process is what I coach women to use as they strive to change their thoughts, body, relationships and ultimately their lives.

We call it the "D.I.V.E. & Create Action Process". Also known as The MindStrength 5 Step process.

As you start to make changes, you will feel resistance and your subconscious mind, in an effort to protect you, will serve up thoughts such as, "This is hard. I don't know if this is worth it." When this happens, just remember that you have made a commitment and you know what you want and your conscious mind is steering the ship now.

When you make mistakes along this path, and you will make many, or when you have doubts and negative thoughts that come up, don't look at these setbacks and negative thoughts as defeat. These setbacks and thoughts are simply feedback that your subconscious mind is uncomfortable with the change, not that you've made the wrong choice and shouldn't continue on the path to change.

When these thoughts come into your mind, I want you to choose to go through the following exercise. The came name of this process is an acronym to assist you in remembering the 5 steps: "D.I.V.E. & Create Action"

Let me put a visual picture in your mind that will hopefully assist you in remembering the acronym. Use each letter in the acronym to pull yourself out of a funk or to correct an old negative pattern that you don't want to experience any more.

If you were standing on top of a tall diving board next to a large pool and the ladder was taken away, what choice would you have? You can D.I.V.E. into the pool and be totally fine or you can try and jump back on to the concrete and experience more pain.

This is essentially what happens when we are faced with a negative thought or make a mistake on our path to creating new beliefs and habits. We get to choose to try and go back to our old ways and experience that pain, or we get to choose to D.I.V.E. & Create Action that will lead us to what we want to experience.

I'll now explain the definition of this acronym so you can walk yourself through this process whenever you have an experience or thought that does not serve you in creating the life, body or relationships you want.

## STEP 1: DEFINE

The Define step is where we define the thoughts that are floating around in our minds, positive or negative. When you don't feel amazing ask these questions:

How am I feeling right now?

What are my negative thoughts?

## STEP 2: INQUIRE

After you go through the "Define" step, you will generally become aware of a few active thoughts. Of those active thoughts, one or more of them are likely negative thoughts. The Inquire step allows you to focus on the cause of the negative thoughts that you have.

What was going on in my mind before this thought or emotion came up?

What was done or said that made me feel this way?

## STEP 3: VALIDATE

In the "Inquire" step you focused on a specific negative thought. In the Validation Step, you analyze the negative thought and what caused it then ask yourself if your reaction or negative thought is an accurate interpretation. You can do this by asking yourself these questions:

Is this thought or perception that came into my mind a true or accurate interpretation of the situation or am I assuming something that is not true?

Is there evidence to support this thought as being true?

## STEP 4: EVALUATE

In the "Validate" step, you asked questions to verify if what you were feeling in regards to the negative thought was true or accurate. In the Evaluate step, you are going to ask God to help you see the truth through His eyes as well as how and what to change.

How would God look down and see this situation?

How would God interpret the thing that caused me to have this negative thought?

## STEP 5: CREATE ACTION

To take us out of our negative thought and replace it, we get to create an action to work on daily when our negative thought comes up. You get to decide what action you will use to replace it. Decide what the specific action is and then act on it daily.

What do I really want?

What's one thing in this situation that I can do which will change my emotion immediately, reinforce my goal and put me back on the path of reaching that goal?

When you begin to make changes, negative thoughts will come up from your subconscious mind to try and keep you on your old path, the path that it still believes you want to be on.

This process is effective in both correcting false beliefs (it's too hard to…) and negative thoughts (I'm fat). This first example is how you might use this process to change a false belief.

A common conversation I used to have in my head when I started changing my eating habits was, "eating healthy takes too much time, thought and preparation and is a LOT of work, I'm not sure it's worth it…".

## Correcting A False Belief: Eating Healthy Is Too Hard

D- I DEFINE the reason I am thinking that eating healthy is hard, time consuming, etc. Well, when I compare it to sticking processed junk in the microwave, or going through the fast food drive-thru… it is more time consuming and does require more thought and preparation.

I- Next, I INQUIRE about why I am feeling that it may not be worth it. This feeling comes when I don't see quick results from eating healthy. When I am not seeing my body change as fast as I want it to, I feel like it's not worth the effort.

V- Then I VALIDATE my thoughts about eating healthy being time consuming, difficult and not worth it. Is that true? While it takes a little more time to plan, prepare and take healthy foods with me when I'm out of the house for extended periods of time, the reality is I do have more energy, I am seeing results and know I will continue to see more of the results I want as I maintain this habit.

E- After that I EVALUATE the situation from God's perspective. I imagine what decision I would make if I was given His perspective on this thought and situation. Would God have me continue planning, preparing and choosing to live healthy or from his perspective should I give in to this feeling that "it's not worth it"? I realize that what I would choose for myself if I were looking from God's perspective is to continue on the path of investing my time and effort into healthy eating. I see through His perspective that as I maintain my path, it will become easier and more natural and I WILL see the physical changes over time.

CREATE ACTION- I now use this new perspective of the situation and CREATE an action plan to get what I truly want. In this case, I choose to simplify my food planning and preparation even more. Looking at what foods I actually enjoy eating and decide to substitute those that I don't with other healthy options. For example, I choose to replace eating broccoli with my lunch meal to eat a pre-mixed salad instead. I then get to do something immediately to reinforce this decision to make eating healthy less of a chore and be reminded of how much better I feel. I start this by writing down my adjusted meal plan that I will enjoy more, even if it's not perfect.

One of the things that often causes us to grab hold of a negative thought or belief are the actions of others. We often "assume" that an action or lack of an expected action by someone we love equates to, "I must not be loved".

However, often this is not at all the intent of our loved one, but merely our perception. Sure, they may have made a mistake or been very insensitive, but rarely is the "meaning" behind it as extreme as "I'm not loved".

"My husband once again failed to do what I was thinking he should do… he must not really love me." Wait, WHAT?!? How do we jump to that conclusion so quickly? Again, it's because of our nature and how we were raised to believe. We give meaning or define situations based on how we were indirectly taught as we grew up.

I've had a belief that is common among many of us, which started for me when I was a child. The belief or thought was "I don't know enough" or "I'm not smart enough". Because of this, when my husband asks me a question that he expects me to know the answer to and I don't, I feel attacked as if he doesn't believe that I know enough and is challenging me.

In this type of situation I used to pull back into my shell and not respond to avoid confrontation or an uncomfortable conversation. Now when something like this occurs in my relationship, I follow this process.

### Correcting A Negative Thought: I Am Not Smart Enough

D- I DEFINE the emotions and thoughts I'm having about being asked something that I don't know the answer to. I recognize I'm feeling judged or not loved by my husband, as if he is challenging me and my knowledge.

I- Next, I INQUIRE about why I am feeling that way. This feeling of judgement comes when I feel he doesn't believe that I know enough about the topic we are discussing.

V- Then I VALIDATE my thoughts about my husband thinking that I don't know enough and ask, is that really how my husband feels about me? No, it probably wasn't his intent to make me feel like I am not smart enough when he asked the question, but I perceived that because of prior experiences I'd had as a young girl. Even if that was his intent, I can choose to see how his judging me to not be smart enough is, in a way, a reflection of his own insecurities and doesn't really mean that, "I'm not smart enough", but means that he feels insecure and took it out on me.

E- I then EVALUATE the situation from the perspective of God and imagine what action He would take to create a positive outcome with this conversation with my husband. God knows that my husband and I are both imperfect. We don't always communicate clearly and I can give my husband the benefit of the doubt in this situation instead of accepting hurt feelings and shutting down or responding with a counter attack. I know my husband loves me, he tells me every day as well as shows it through daily acts of service, such as doing dishes (which he does because he knows I hate doing dishes), playing with the kids and helping out around the house. He would do anything for me, so I get to choose to share with him how his question made me feel and allow him to express what his true intent was. If my husband has shown malicious intent in the past in this type of situation, then I would look at this from God's perspective in this way: The truth is that my husband is a Son of God. He is not perfect and he is obviously hurting if he is lashing out at me this way. What would allow my husband to open up and share what is causing him to lash out in this way?

CREATE ACTION- I now use this new perspective of the situation and CREATE a positive outcome by telling my husband, "When you asked me X, it made me feel like you are judging me and that you feel like I don't know enough". I then get to have this authentic conversation with my husband and allow him to express his true feelings (which are almost always much more positive than my negative assumption) and we get to create a healthier relationship with authentic communication.

If my husband had been malicious, then I would create action by letting him know that I felt very hurt by his response and I imagine he is feeling hurt as well. I would ask him in a calm and loving way, "What are you feeling or what is making you feel hurt?". He most likely will not respond authentically the first time or even the first few times, but if I continue to show genuine love and compassion, seeing him through God's eyes, he will eventually, over time, open up. Most men are good at their core, but have learned to close off emotionally if they feel they've been hurt or their trust has been violated in the past when they tried being vulnerable.

I've seen a huge improvement in myself and my confidence to speak up for what needs to be said because I've applied this process into my life daily. It may not come easy at first, but nothing ever does, but over time you will feel more comfortable going through this process and can do it in your head in a matter of a minute or two and get back on to creating a new default reaction to situations and thoughts.

# CHAPTER 10

# CONNECTION & GREAT SEX

# CONNECTION & GREAT SEX

Every woman wants an amazing, connected relationship with a good man who honors, loves and cherishes her. Sadly, this is the hope and dream most women lose over the years of marriage. It happened to me as I lost myself in my children and focused solely on them. I was so consumed with caring for my children that I didn't feel like I knew Trent any more and I didn't feel attracted to him.

One of the greatest tools I ever learned, to assist me in creating my ideal life and marriage, was how to be authentic and vulnerable. Together they strengthen relationships.

What is Authenticity?

Unfortunately, most of us have been trained to show up in masks, to appear to be "perfect", or act as others expect us to act in order to be accepted and loved.

Authenticity is existing without hiding behind a mask. Allowing total honesty, as is, the original and raw you. Authenticity is the gift of heartfelt honesty and committing to expressing your thoughts openly in the moment and allowing others to do the same. It gives the incredible (although scary at first) gift of vulnerability.

In relationships, when we are not willing to share what we are feeling and thinking, we are not able to connect at the deepest level.

In 2013 Trent and I learned how not allowing ourselves to be authentic and vulnerable for the first eleven years together almost cost us our marriage. It was the hardest year of our marriage by far. Sure, we had our ups and downs the first decade, but from late 2012 to mid 2013, things went downhill quick.

For the first time in our marriage we were experiencing difficult times financially. Although our income was still well above average, our spending and lifestyle hadn't adjusted quick enough and we had no savings left. We had just moved from California (our home the first 12 years of marriage) and Trent had started working in a new business, but this time as more of an employee/minority owner (another first, as he'd never had a salary job). With the stress of long hours and less income, we were both on edge.

We both found ourselves frustrated with our relationship. Trent would leave the house before 6am and get home often after 7pm. I resented him for being gone so much. I was closed off both physically and emotionally and felt my attraction to him dwindling each month. This feeling was obvious to Trent and made him more depressed each day as he yearned for connection, but also felt like any previous connection was gone from our marriage. It didn't help that he was already feeling a high level of stress from working hard to provide for our family and working longer hours with little to show for it.

Trent felt like he wasn't a good husband or father as he wasn't providing the lifestyle we had become accustomed to. He connected his worth and value to me to his earning ability. He believed that he was not loved or loveable if he couldn't provide a certain level of income and lifestyle.

On a summer day in July when Trent had a day off of work, he had got so down on himself, from the stresses of work, the lack of support and connection he felt at home, that he had a mental breakdown.

This was the scariest day of my life. I had known Trent to always be positive, optimistic, a goal setter and goal achiever. A driven and motivated man. I didn't realize back then how much of his drive and motivation came from wanting to please me, all the while I had been showing him signs of not being happy at all with our circumstances and his lack of time at home.

That morning, Trent was laying in bed until past noon, just staring at a blank wall. He was laying there, depressed, staring and not talking for hours. I eventually got him to leave the house with the family, but the whole time he just sat and stared. He seemed to be completely checked out and the thought entered my mind, "is this the end of our marriage?"

That night, after a full day of blank stares and just a few words from his mouth, we drove alone to a parking lot next to a public park so the two of us could talk. I'll always remember the conversation we had as it was scary, painful and our first attempt at being truly authentic.

We shared our real, raw thoughts and feelings. I even expressed that I wasn't feeling attracted to him anymore and that I felt we had grown apart the last year. We talked about the things that we both had kept buried in our hearts and minds for years. We finally started to discuss our hidden selves. The side that exists in our dark thoughts.

Eventually we talked about what we both truly wanted. We both wanted happiness and deep connection. Neither of us wanted to give up on the other, but we knew we were far from where we wanted to be.

While I hated the feelings and thoughts I had that day and while the pain we both experienced was worse than we'd ever experienced before, it was literally the start of a new relationship.

From that day until today, our marriage has continued to grow and blossom. I can't express the level of love and connection that we've since created as we went through several more months of authentic and often painful conversations to get to know and discover each other all over again. It truly feels like we have a new marriage and a new bond that is stronger than what I had ever imagined was possible.

The lesson we learned from this experience is that you never will fully connect with others until you allow full authenticity and (often painful) vulnerability to exist.

Vulnerability means you are ok allowing others to see that you don't have your life all together and perfect. It means you are willing to share your fears and feelings and quick to acknowledge your mistakes, knowing that the other person could use that information to hurt you. This requires the highest level of trust and is very uncomfortable for most people at first. Until this level of trust exists with your most intimate relationships, there will always be a lack of connection. This is not only true in your marriage, but in your other close relationships with family and your best friends.

After that horrible day, as Trent and I first started practicing being authentic and vulnerable, it was really hard to open up and be honest as we didn't like how vulnerable we felt.

As a man, Trent wanted so much to maintain the 'hero' status in our marriage. He wanted to appear as a man without flaws, not having anything wrong with him that would reveal weaknesses for a fear that I wouldn't love him if I knew all the things he dealt with.

I on the other hand just didn't want to know that my husband had weaknesses and feared what he would think of me if he knew of my struggles and so we resisted being authentic.

In order for you to get to this raw level of vulnerability in your marriage, it requires you to both work towards a deep level of unconditional self-love and approval. You must be okay with your dark side of you as well as your light side. Accepting of your weaknesses and knowledge that you nor your spouse is perfect.

This requires you to be non-judgmental and to see your spouse through God's eyes and recognize that you are both broken in some way and must fully rely on the atonement of our Savior to be made whole. Neither one of you is better than the other, we are equal in that way.

The truth is, the only way to create the deepest level of connection with your spouse is to stop pretending to have it all together. Since Trent was able to drop the mask and I know the real, imperfect man that he is, he has become so much more attractive to me. I see it as a strength for him to open up his heart and expose himself in his truest form, trusting me fully to not hurt him. When I became more vulnerable, Trent also noticed an increased attraction for me. He said it added to my "sexy confidence" and he felt more connected to me than at any time in our marriage.

## PROPER COMMUNICATION = AMAZING CONNECTION

Once I learned that communication solves every problem, whether with your spouse, children, business, or life, I finally understood SEX.

It had to take someone outside of our marriage (Bri & Tony Litster) to walk us through what we were

Trent and I in October, 2014

feeling. We listened intently to what they had to share and how their lack of understanding for the other person's thoughts and feelings created a deep divide in their relationship.

It wasn't for a lack of wanting to understand, but a lack of knowing how to communicate effectively. We were able to work with them to find a way out of what I thought was just my mess in my head. I was the one who was holding us back from fully connecting sexually in our marriage because I didn't want to talk about it. Stuff you don't talk about usually doesn't change.

I finally made the choice to change. I didn't want to be an uninvolved participant in the act of sex as I had done during most of our marriage. I wanted to experience the pleasure that he was every time we had sex, not just occasionally. I finally chose to see it as something for ME to enjoy with him and not just something I had to do for HIM!

I have a few tips that transformed my view on sex that I'd like to share. You may not be in the same situation I was in, some of you have no problem in this area and others are far worse off than I was, but we can all improve on connecting more fully.

First, I finally chose to be open to read and learn more, from good sources, about the benefits to sex in a marriage. As I read about how sex, as a tool for connection, worked I wanted to experience those things in my marriage.

A few things that I was drawn to were that sex increases your mental clarity and creativity, it enhances your self-esteem and makes you look and feel younger.

Another thing that helped me to have more desire to feel pleasure during sex was understanding my anatomy as a woman. I shut down whenever I heard anything about my body as a source of pleasure for so long, that I didn't know much about these wondrous parts of my body that are used for sex and pleasure. I began to learn and understand the power and benefit of these "undiscovered" parts of my body.

I came to learn that sex is the anchor that connects Trent and I and that it's the core foundation of a healthy marriage. That is the only thing that we exclusively share together. We both wanted a great marriage and we knew that sex was the core element in creating that.

Trent and I found what works for us and we began to talk to each other during and after intimacy to find what works and what doesn't to create more pleasure and a better connection during intimacy. We now feel like our needs are being met and can confidently express what we want during this intimate time together.

## FREE RESOURCE:

Trent and I recorded a video together in which we discuss the challenges we faced in our sexual connection and what assisted us in creating deeper connection through intimacy. To watch this video on your smartphone or computer, text the word **INTIMACY** to **(877) 858-1510** and I'll send you the video link.

You don't realize how much this knowledge about sex has changed my life! I still have my moments of not wanting to connect, but I now have tools to set me up to move through it to create the connection that can come through intimacy. I am wanting this connection more than ever before.

When we finally had made this change, after over 10 years of marriage and being in a place of poor communication and frustration, we decided that we wanted to create an epic marriage. Our commitment to that decision brought us to this point of amazing connection through authenticity, vulnerability and great sex.

An epic marriage is one where there is a deep lasting emotional, physical and intellectual connection that allows there to be lasting fulfillment and intimacy that grows with time.

One of my mentors, Gerald Rogers, said this of an epic marriage:

"An epic marriage requires a mindset that includes unconditional love, commitment, trust, forgiveness, working as a team, and a willingness to choose 'in' and do the daily work of nurturing the marriage over and over again. An epic marriage requires the skills of positive communication, true intimacy, cooperation, and compromise, effective money management, parenting skills, and knowing how to really give and receive love."

I make a choice each and everyday to make my marriage epic, as Gerald has so eloquently described it. It requires awareness of how I am feeling and recognizing what Trent is feeling too.

I've worked with and mentored clients who were either happily married or in marriages on the verge of divorce. When they go through The MindStrength Transformational Program, (my 10 week program) and have a spouse who is also committed to an epic marriage, there is the opportunity for a complete shift into the most amazing relationships.

As with any relationship, it takes two people to create one that works, but you can have a dramatic impact on creating the change necessary to have the relationship you've always wanted. Trust me ladies. Your man wants to feel loved and appreciated and he wants you. If he feels connected to you, he will slay dragons for you. Choose to create this in your relationship.

## CHAPTER 11

# FAIL PROOF WAY TO CREATE CHANGE

# FAIL PROOF WAY TO CREATE CHANGE

Change isn't easy and it isn't quick. Of course, you can decide today to start a new workout program or meal plan and be perfect at it for a few days. However, after 3 weeks on a new program, most people have already decided the effort is no longer worth the long term reward and they've abandoned their original plan. Don't believe me? Go to your gym in January and again in March and you'll notice that more than half of the "January" crowd are no longer there in March. In fact, it's closer to 80% that are no longer there.

This happens to all of us in different areas of life. Here are a few reasons why it's hard to stick to our plans to change, even when we start with the best of intentions and a ton of motivation.

The 3 main reasons why we don't stick to new plans long enough for the actions to become easy to maintain habits are:

1- We have a limited supply of willpower each day.

2- Motivation comes and goes and when it's gone, it's very hard to keep on the plan that we created at the height of our motivation.

3- We all lack confidence when we start something that is new to us. This lack of confidence makes us more likely to throw in the towel, as things don't go so smooth during our first few days or weeks of doing this new thing.

Let's go over these one by one and learn about how we can turn the tables on these main causes of failure. As examples, we'll use starting a new workout and meal plan.

## WILLPOWER

Willpower is a fascinating thing. I'm not going to go into all the science behind it in this book. You can find plenty of recently published books on the subject, but here is what I've learned (so you can save yourself a few hours of reading).

Willpower is used up during the day whenever we make decisions, even if they don't seem to be "difficult" decisions. Any decision making will drain your willpower reserve. Even something as simple as, "What color shirt should I wear today?"

Willpower is replenished by both food (specifically glucose) and sleep.

Willpower, like a muscle, can be strengthened over time with focused use.

Because willpower can be depleted, it is unreliable and should not be your primary tool for creating lasting change.

## MOTIVATION

Motivation is fickle. It comes and goes and is an even less reliable tool for creating lasting change than willpower. Can you think of something that you were recently so passionate about doing that you researched online, read every book, bought several products related to it and invested much of your free time into it?

Then, just a few weeks (or maybe months) later, your motivation had dissipated so much that you could care less about that thing or topic? That's the bad thing about motivation. If it's the only thing driving you to start on a new meal plan or exercise routine, you'll almost certainly be over it in a few weeks when your motivation dips. You will have eventually stopped the healthy habits that you so passionately started at the beginning. Sound familiar?

## CONFIDENCE

Confidence is learned through experience. How did you feel the first time you walked into a gym and attempted to use some of the equipment? Awkward? Worried about looking foolish in front of others? When we lack confidence, it affects our motivation in a big way and can also trump our willpower to do the thing that we committed to.

Confidence does not come without effort and focused intent. We gain confidence through increased competency and repetition.

## HOW TO CREATE LASTING CHANGE

How do we efficiently use our willpower, maintain a high level of motivation and quickly increase our confidence for long enough to actually create lasting change?

The key to maintaining willpower is to make less decisions throughout your day. By using less of your willpower during the course of the day, there is more of it available to you when you see that late night snack that would normally tempt you beyond what you are able to resist.

For example, if you are starting a new meal plan that has normally been difficult for you to stick to, the following would make you use less willpower and increase your odds of actually sticking to it long enough to create a healthy habit:

- Choose your clothes for the week, including your exercise clothes.

- Eat the same breakfast every day.

- Pick a day each week and prepare all of your lunches for the week.

- Have your snacks prepared and accessible for the week.

- Have a weekly dinner plan so you know ahead of time what you'll be preparing/eating each night.

- Decide in advance what foods you choose not to eat so you don't even need to decide.

The less you have to THINK and CHOOSE, the less willpower you use up throughout the day and the more likely it is that you will be consistent in creating the new habit.

Even when you use less willpower, you still are limited by your level of motivation to create change. The key to sustained motivation is community. When you are part of a community, you are much more likely to maintain a high level of motivation.

I have identified three primary reasons why being part of a community is so important to creating lasting change:

First, there is implied accountability to other members the community.

Second, the continued curiosity and new information that comes from being part of a group of like minded people keeps you interested.

Finally, as you see others reaping the benefits of the lifestyle, your motivation stays high and you maintain hope to achieve the outcome you want.

I'll clarify how this works by using an example, think back to any club or organization you've been a part of. I think of my church as a perfect example for this. As I attend my church weekly, meet with like minded people who have a common interest and common goals, it is much easier for me to stay motivated each day to live the life that I commit to as part of the membership in my church. We unite in common morals and standards and as I see others around me reaping the benefits of living this lifestyle, my motivation remains high, in spite of setbacks that will occur in my life.

The final key to increase your likelihood of lasting change is by finding a mentor or someone who has "been there, done that" to give you the confidence during those crucial first few weeks of creating change.

Look for someone who understands where you are and can empathetically help you gain confidence as you learn new daily practices that will create the outcome you want. I have been blessed to assist women one on one and in small groups through my MindStrength Transformational Program (a 10 week interactive program).

I have been where you are. Either not feeling good enough, not feeling connected in your most important relationships or living in an unhealthy body. I know what path is most likely to create lasting change.

## ACTION STEPS:

To summarize, here is what makes long lasting change more likely and what keeps people on their plan, until it becomes easy and effortless.

1- Identify ways to reduce the decisions you make each day. Create a plan and chunk together activities such as food prep so you aren't having to make decisions as often. This also relates to any decision you make in a day, not just health related decisions.

2- Be part of a community. Join a group with common goals and seek out a mentor (often you can find a mentor and community in one). Those who have already gone down the same path you are on can work with you through your lows and assist you in keeping the motivation to create what you really do want in your life. The community and your mentors help you to see that the results you are after are possible to attain.

3- Learn from someone else who has walked the path you are going down in order to reduce your learning curve. A mentor or someone from your community can really help to boost your confidence and dramatically impact your chances of creating lasting change. They can assist you in becoming competent in creating daily routines that lead to the life and results you are after. Competency and repetition create confidence.

# CHAPTER 12

# NOT TODAY

# NOT TODAY

Here's the dirty little secret about creating habits and changing your thoughts, body, relationships, and results.

It doesn't happen right away!

Change is not going to happen today, just because you decided it would.

There is this terribly false idea that goes around in the "fat loss" community. They hype and sell people on these "lose 30 pounds in 30 days" programs and lead you to believe that results always come quickly. This has led to unfair expectations that we'll see "results" in a matter of days… otherwise we must be broken!

It's a lie! Be patient.

Trust that as you create and maintain habits that other healthy people have, you too will soon enough be healthy. If you create and maintain the habits of people in amazing relationships, you will soon enough create amazing relationships!

We all understand where this comes from. Our society has created the illusion that instant gratification is possible. Society says, "I want it now. I want to change everything and I want to change today!" The truth is, lasting change is slow, but is not as difficult when we focus on changing one thing at a time.

Here is the real secret to my success, when things finally clicked for me. I focused on gaining confidence in just one area of my life and creating change in just one area. This narrow focus combined with the support of a community of great people made all the difference.

There was one thing that I did different, when I finally broke through my past 'start and stop cycle' of exercise and eating healthier. What was different when I finally had a breakthrough was that I had coaches, mentors and cheerleaders. I didn't try and do it all alone. I had people who walked me through my negative thoughts to see that they were false and who showed me through their results that if I kept going, I too could have the same results.

These were people who lifted me when I felt weak. Mentors who I knew I had to report to on my training, meals, relationships and more. This held me accountable at a MUCH higher level than had I tried to rely on my willpower and motivation to hold myself accountable.

Not only did I hire mentors, but I was part of a group of other women on the same path as me. This helped me tremendously in getting past those hard times during those first couple months of creating change. Relying on my sisters who were on the same path and listening to my mentors allowed me to finally uncover the confident, capable, loving, optimistic Sarah that had been hidden for so long! Once I had shifted my thought patterns, I became what my husband calls "sexy confident".

I was able to shine as a daughter of God and others, besides my husband, began to notice. Women at my church and at my gym began approaching me and asking my what had changed. This was proof to me that I truly had made lasting change this time. Not only did I notice, but those who knew me could tell too.

My point is that you can do it. You can change. No matter how many times you've tried and failed in the past, there is hope for you this time.

There is a science to change and until now, you may have relied too much on your own self, your own willpower, your own motivation and your own experiences to try and figure out the path to get to where you want to be.

Even if you feel you've tried and had all the support you needed, I can tell you that there is likely something else that is holding you back. You would benefit from discussing your inner beliefs and feelings about why change is hard for you. Find a mentor or someone who has been where you are and can help you see the truth and identify what has been holding you back from the peace and happiness you desire.

Ask yourself these questions:

How many times have I tried and failed?

Is it possible that I might fail again if I try again?

What can I do this time, to support me in actually getting through those hard times?

What will help me to address those false beliefs that I may not even be aware of and to create the confidence that I know is hidden within?

Write down whatever action ideas you came up with. These promptings should be acted upon as soon as possible.

Remember, change will happen over time. If you expect a smokin' hot body in just 4-6 weeks, it most likely isn't going to happen.

However, if you do the things daily that healthy people do, over the next few months and year you will see a big change! Consistency, realistic expectations and focus on the short term benefits will assist you with the daily motivation to keep you on this path. Don't forget the value of a community in keeping you focused and your level of motivation high.

Because change doesn't happen as fast as we want, we can get frustrated. One of the women I coached told me she felt like the MindStrength Transformational Program wasn't doing anything for her. This came up during a one-on-one call about 3 or 4 weeks into the Program. She was questioning if the daily practices were even worth doing as she didn't feel any different and wasn't seeing change.

I walked her through those thoughts and gave her some tools to help her as they came up. I then gave her examples of other people who had also felt the same way, but who had kept going and achieved the results that she was after. I asked her to trust the process for a couple more weeks and allow time and consistency to take effect in creating change.

A few weeks later, after remaining consistent to the daily practices we were working on, she began to notice a difference in her natural response to thoughts, emotions and situations. After just 2-3 months, she was a totally different woman and had transformed her beliefs about her self worth.

This woman has said on multiple occasions that she feels totally confident now and is addressing issues in her life that would have never been resolved otherwise.

Now instead of worrying about people looking at her and judging her when she is out in public, she no longer worries about what others might be thinking. Her confidence allows her to now remain consistent in her positive daily habits with much less effort.

MindStrength is all about creating confidence. Confidence can be 'borrowed' from our success in other areas of our lives. As we set ourselves up for success to change just one thing in our life, we soon feel confident in that area in a way we may not have imagined possible.

We then leverage that success and confidence to create a domino effect and we get to work on the next "most impactful" change to create even more confidence. Slowly, but surely, we become "sexy confident" and we begin to no longer compare ourselves or even worry about what others 'might be thinking' and instead we think about what else we can create in our lives, bodies and relationships.

# CHAPTER 13

# TAKE ACTION

# TAKE ACTION

What have you been feeling as you've read these words?

Have you read something in this book that has made you feel uncomfortable?

"You" meaning you. Not the collective "you" who may pick up this book, but you - the individual, courageous, beautiful, strong woman who is reading this book right now.

Not all things can be taught by reading a book. Each of us is unique. I hope the things which I have identified as the most common will allow you to challenge old beliefs and follow a process to create new patterns and habits.

Take the leap! What if today is the day that everything changes? You were created for a purpose. You don't need the perfect circumstances or timing or title to make what matters happen. Use what you have, where you are and DIVE in! Send it, start it, say it, make the call, let it go, take that risk! Today is the day to make it happen!

My hope is that you will follow the action list below and start on the path to create the body, relationships and life that YOU want. Allowing yourself to become sexy confident and become a beacon of light for the women in your life.

Don't just set this book aside and check it off your list as "read". Take action quickly on what you have felt inspired to do.

"Finish each day and be done with it," wrote Ralph Waldo Emerson. "You have done what you could. Some blunders and absurdities no doubt crept in; forget them as soon as you can. Tomorrow is a new day; begin it well and serenely."

Emerson reminds us that each new day is a gift, a new beginning, a fresh start. And each NEW day, whether sunny or snowy, overcast or clear, is a chance to commence the journey of life. Yes, at times that journey seems all uphill— such journeys are best approached one day at a time. And as we do, a new day can turn into a new week, a new year, a new life.

Someone once told me, "Wait until the morning to make important decisions. Don't make them at night." I've thought about this and questioned, "Why wait until morning?"

It's because a new day can cast encouraging light on yesterday's troubles. We can start the day with a positive outlook, some inner strength, and exercise faith in God and our hope will be renewed and we will see opportunities before us.

We may not always see the sunshine right away. Some days start out cloudy and seem to only get darker. But if we can look forward with some hope and a bit of confidence, then each day can be a wonderful day.

So look for the sunshine. Watch for the wonder. Try to make each day the kind of day you want to remember.

I've created a new and deeper perspective on my own life and feel so grateful to take my life one day at a time.

I've overcome many obstacles that don't stand in my way anymore because I believe I'm worth it.

**And so are YOU! One Day at a Time.**

# APPENDIX

# ACTION CHECKLIST & RESOURCES

# ACTION CHECKLIST

1. Each morning, perform the "Love Yourself from the Inside Out" exercise from Page 38. Text **INSIDE** to (877) 858-1510 to get the detailed instructions on how to do this.

2. Take time to decide what you really want and set goals in the 5 areas described on Page 47

3. Also on Page 47, identify what daily rituals you can create to assist you in believing that you are worthy of achieving the goals you set.

4. On Page 49 we talk about recognizing your blessings and the things you already do well. Don't skip this, it's crucial!

5. Determine the habits and actions that lead to the goals you set for yourself, as described on Page 50.

6. Follow the DIVE & Create Action process in Chapter 9 to overcome the daily negative thoughts that are holding you back.

7. Text the word **INTIMACY** to **(877) 858-1510** and watch the video of my husband and I. Take time to watch this and discuss with your spouse, if you are married.

8. Go through the Action Items at the end of Chapter 11 on page 96.

9. Determine how to use less willpower by making less decisions each day (prepare ahead of time, so your habits don't require you to make many decision).

10. Find a community of people who are on your same path or who have the results you are after to assist you with ongoing motivation and accountability.

11. Seek out a mentor or coach who has experience helping people get the result you are after. They will assist you in overcoming your thoughts and reduce your learning curve as they help you avoid the mistakes that most people on your path make. A mentor or coach will greatly increase your likelihood of achieving your desired outcome or goal.

# RESOURCES

To get additional MindStrength Resources, visit the MindStrength website at: **http://MindStrengthMentor.com**

Send a text message for information on these additional resources.

The MindStrength 5 Step Process:
**\*Text PROCESS to (877) 858-1510**

The MindStrength Transformational Experience:
**\*Text EXPERIENCE to (877) 858-1510**

The MindStrength Mamas Community:
**\*Text COMMUNITY to (877) 858-1510**

\*STANDARD DATA FEES AND TEXT MESSAGING RATES MAY APPLY

Made in the USA
San Bernardino, CA
21 April 2015